by Janie Scheffer

BLASTOFF! READERS, AN IMPRINT OF BELLWETHER MEDIA BY FLUTTERBEE

Blastoff! Readers are carefully developed by literacy experts to build reading stamina and move students toward fluency by combining standards-based content with developmentally appropriate text.

Level 1 provides the most support through repetition of high-frequency words, light text, predictable sentence patterns, and strong visual support.

Level 2 offers early readers a bit more challenge through varied sentences, increased text load, and text-supportive special features.

Level 3 advances early-fluent readers toward fluency through increased text load, less reliance on photos, advancing concepts, longer sentences, and more complex special features.

★ **Blastoff! Universe**

Reading Level

Blastoff! Beginners — Grade K

Grades 1–3

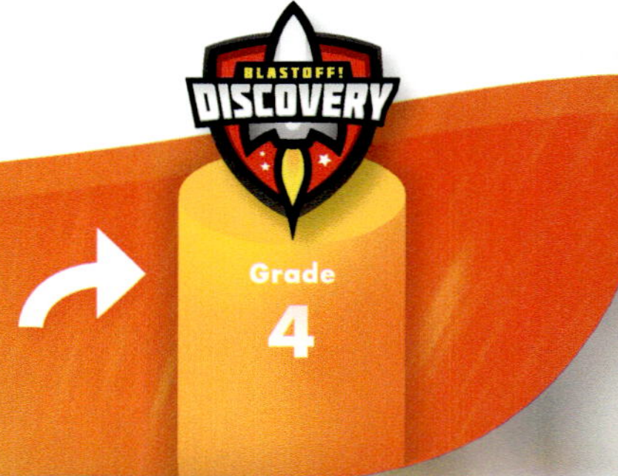

Grade 4

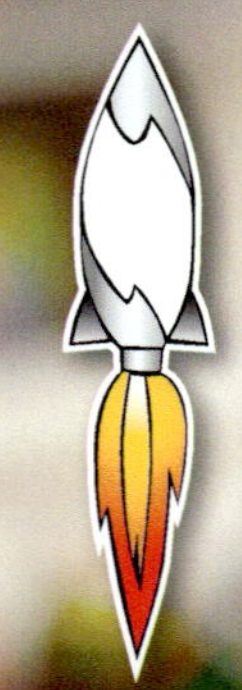

This edition first published in 2027 by Bellwether Media, Inc.

For information regarding permission, write to Bellwether Media, Inc., Attention: Permissions Department, 3500 American Blvd W, Suite 150, Bloomington, MN 55431.

Names: Scheffer, Janie, 1992- author
Title: Shapes / by Janie Scheffer.
Description: Blastoff! readers. | Minneapolis, Minnesota : Bellwether Media, Inc, 2027. | Series: Fun with math | Includes bibliographical references and index. | Audience: Ages 5-8 | Audience: Grades 2-3 | Summary: "Relevant images match informative text in this introduction to shapes. Intended for students in kindergarten through third grade"-- Provided by publisher.
Identifiers: LCCN 2026011451 (print) | LCCN 2026011452 (ebook) | ISBN 9798898800550 library binding | ISBN 9798898802967 paperback | ISBN 9798898801793 ebook
Subjects: LCSH: Shapes
Classification: LCC QA445.5 .S365 2027 (print) | LCC QA445.5 (ebook) | DDC 516/.15--dc23/eng/20260319
LC record available at https://lccn.loc.gov/2026011451
LC ebook record available at https://lccn.loc.gov/2026011452

Editor: Rebecca Sabelko Designer: Brittany McIntosh

Printed in the United States of America, North Mankato, MN.

Table of Contents

What Are Shapes?

I am at the playground. I run to the tire swing and climb on.

My legs are in the middle.
I know this shape!

What Shape Do You See?

See answer on page 23!

Shapes are the outside lines of objects. They **define** objects. They help people understand objects.

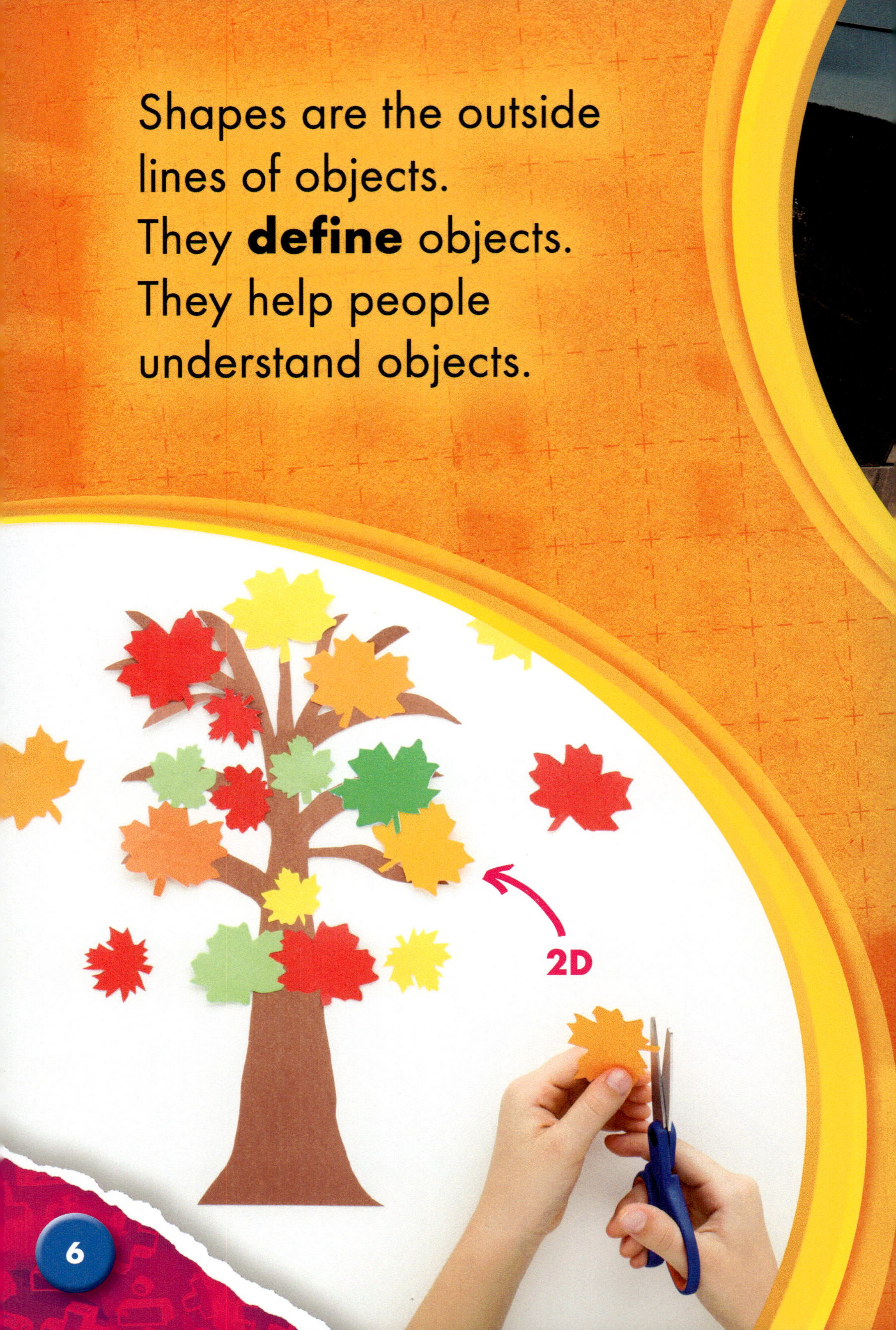

Some shapes are **two-dimensional**, or 2D. Others are **three-dimensional**, or 3D.

Two-dimensional shapes are flat. They have a length and a **height**.

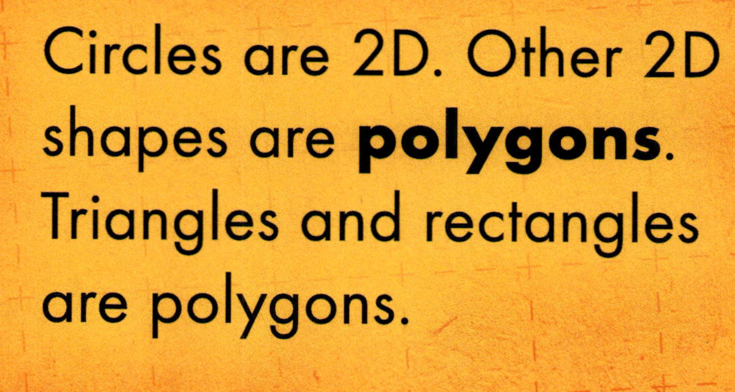

Circles are 2D. Other 2D shapes are **polygons**. Triangles and rectangles are polygons.

triangle

Three-dimensional shapes are **solid** objects. They have a length, a width, and a height.

Spheres, cubes, and cones are 3D. They take up space.

Working with Shapes

People can use tools to make 2D shapes. **Rulers** help people draw shapes with straight lines.

People use **compasses** to draw circles.

ruler

compass

Many objects are 3D shapes. A ball is a sphere. A drinking glass is a cylinder.

People eat ice cream from cones.

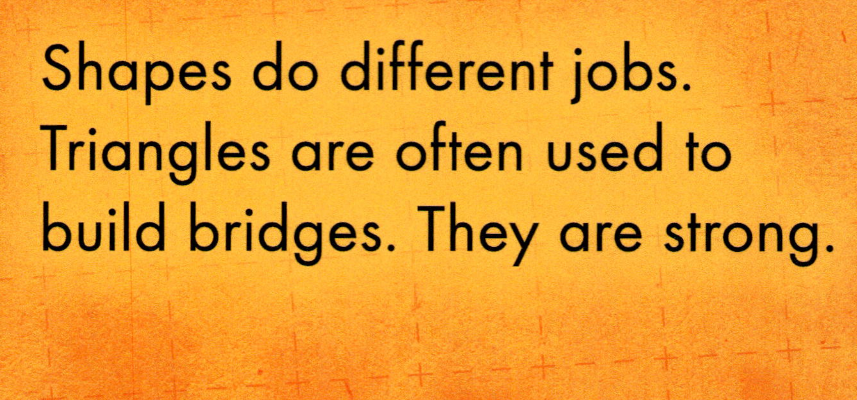

Shapes do different jobs. Triangles are often used to build bridges. They are strong.

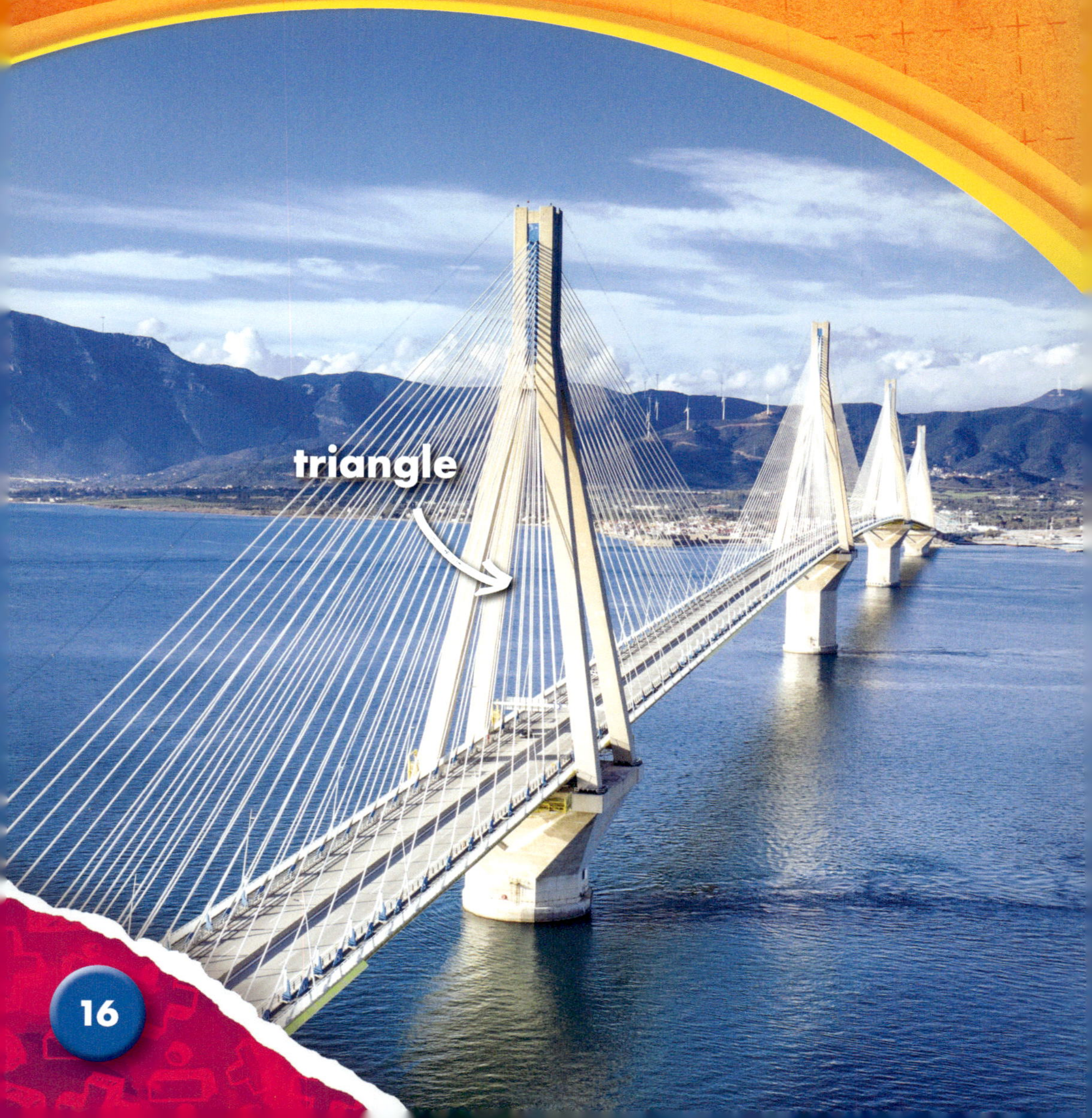

triangle

Circles are used to build things that move. They roll easily.

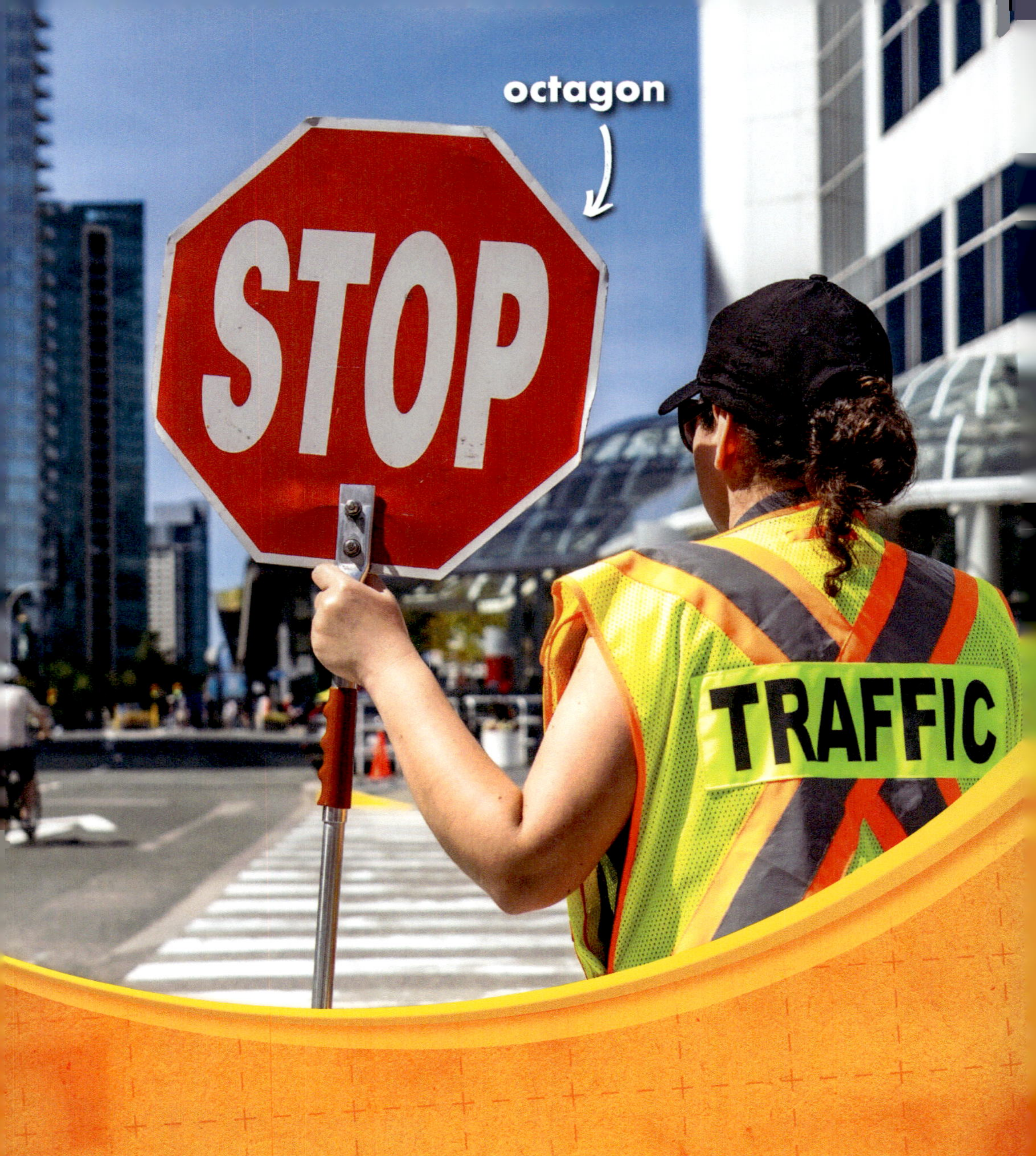

Shapes can also keep us safe. Red octagons are stop signs.

Warning signs are often yellow triangles. They tell us to watch out!

Shapes help people understand objects and spaces every day.

They are an important part of the world!

Glossary

compasses–instruments with two hinged legs that are used for drawing circles

define–to determine the limits or extent of

height–the distance from the bottom to the top

polygons–closed, flat shapes with straight lines and at least three sides

rulers–straight pieces of wood, metal, or plastic that are marked off in inches or other units and are used for measuring length

solid–having a three-dimensional form

three-dimensional–related to solid objects that have a length, a width, and a height

two-dimensional–related to flat shapes that have a length and a width

To Learn More

AT THE LIBRARY

Chytilová, Lenka. *Shapes, Shapes Everywhere.* Prague, Czech Republic: Albatros Media, 2023.

Hokkanen, Mirka. *Kitty and Cat: Bent Out of Shape.* Somerville, Mass.: Candlewick Press, 2023.

Narayan, Anita. *Art Trouble: Art + Math = Cool Things!* Philadelphia, Penn.: The Kinder Cookie Press, 2024.

ON THE WEB

FACTSURFER

Factsurfer.com gives you a safe, fun way to find more information.

1. Go to www.factsurfer.com.
2. Enter "shapes" into the search box and click 🔍.
3. Select your book cover to see a list of related content.

The answer to the question on page 5 is a circle!

Index

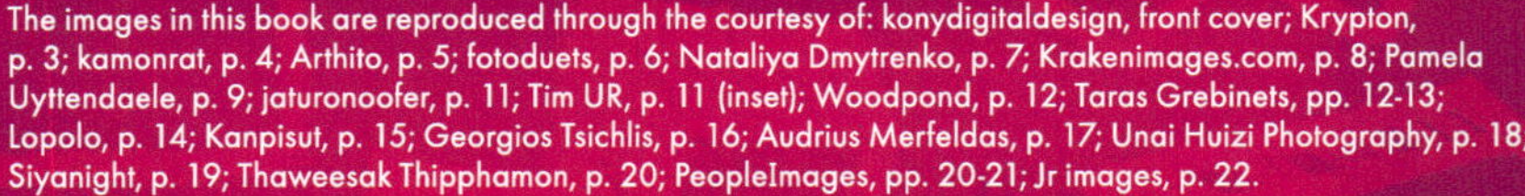

The images in this book are reproduced through the courtesy of: konydigitaldesign, front cover; Krypton, p. 3; kamonrat, p. 4; Arthito, p. 5; fotoduets, p. 6; Nataliya Dmytrenko, p. 7; Krakenimages.com, p. 8; Pamela Uyttendaele, p. 9; jaturonoofer, p. 11; Tim UR, p. 11 (inset); Woodpond, p. 12; Taras Grebinets, pp. 12-13; Lopolo, p. 14; Kanpisut, p. 15; Georgios Tsichlis, p. 16; Audrius Merfeldas, p. 17; Unai Huizi Photography, p. 18; Siyanight, p. 19; Thaweesak Thipphamon, p. 20; PeopleImages, pp. 20-21; Jr images, p. 22.